Psalms

FOR YOUNG CHILDREN

Marie-Hélène Delval ✦ Arno

Psalms

FOR YOUNG CHILDREN

Eerdmans Books for Young Readers

Grand Rapids, Michigan ✦ Cambridge, U.K.

This selection of Psalms, paraphrased for young readers, uses language and imagery appropriate for children while remaining faithful to the spirit of the biblical texts.

When I listen to you, God,
when I do what you ask me to,
I am like a tree
planted by a river,
a tree full of fruit
with leaves that are always green.

Psalm 1

God, when I'm in my bed at night, I think about you. And then I'm not scared of anything. I can fall asleep quietly and in peace.

Psalm 4

From the time that I
wake up, God, I talk to you.
You listen to me
and protect me.
You know that I love you!

Psalm 5

People are so small
next to you, God.
You put the stars and the moon
in the sky, and the birds in the air
above the cows and horses in the fields,
and the fish that swim in the seas.
You created all the beauty
in the world!

Psalm 8

God, I thank you with all my
heart for the wonderful things you
do. When I am scared, you are
always there to comfort me.
I am so happy that
I sing about how good
you are to me.

Psalm 9

Sometimes, when I'm very sad,
I worry that you will
forget about me, God.
But then I remember that
you love me always.
So I will sing and be happy!

Psalm 13

God is like a rock,
strong and powerful.
God is like a warm, dry place
during a storm.
He protects me from
things that might hurt me.
When I ask for God's help,
I feel safe.

Psalm 18

God is my shepherd.
He leads me in the right
direction. And even if I have to
walk in a dark place,
I am not scared.
I know nothing will hurt me
if I walk with God!

Psalm 23

God, you protect me.
You are like a shining light
in the darkness. With you,
I am not scared.
I want to live in your house, God.
I want you to teach me
the right way to live.

Psalm 27

God, can you hear me calling out?
Listen to me,
I'm crying for you!
I know that you are not deaf;
I know you can hear me.
Already, in my heart,
I'm saying thank you for listening.

Psalm 28

When I do something wrong,
I tell you about it, God.
And when you forgive me,
I feel calm again.

Psalm 32

I will pray to God
every day of my life.
I want others to know
how great God is; I want
others to sing to God with me.
With God, I have everything
that I need. With God,
nothing is missing.

Psalm 34

A thirsty deer looks for water,
for a river to drink from.
I need God that way.
I'm thirsty inside.
God, send me your light,
show me the way to your house,
high on your mountain!

Psalm 42

If the ground starts to shake,
if the mountains break into pieces
and fall in the sea,
if the waves grow big as giants,
I'm not scared.
God is with me.
God provides a safe place
for me to hide.

Psalm 46

Let's clap our hands
and shout with joy, because
God is a great strong king!
Blow the trumpet for our king!
God is king of all the earth.
Let's celebrate with songs!

Psalm 47

When I do something wrong,
forgive me, God.
I want to feel like
I've just been washed in clean water.
I want to be like brand-new snow.
I feel so happy when you forgive me!

Psalm 51

When I lie in bed,
awake after bedtime,
God, I think about you.
And then I feel warm and calm,
like a baby bird
that snuggles in its mother's wings.

Psalm 63

When I am sad,
it feels like I'm underwater,
like I'm stuck in the mud,
or at the bottom
of a dark hole.
Pull me from this dark place,
God!
Save me! I need your help!

Psalm 69

Help me, God,
I am worried!
Please hurry up!
I know that you are strong.
You are the only one who
can help me.

Psalm 70

Like a mama bird
who has found
a nest for her baby chicks,
God, you provide
a safe, warm place
for me, your child.

Psalm 84

Please don't be angry with me, God,
even if I did do something wrong!
Please show me that you love me.
I want to feel happy again.

Psalm 85

God, you are good
and you forgive me.
You are full of love.
When I pray to you,
I know you will answer me;
I know you will show me
the right path to take.

Psalm 86

God, please listen to me.
I am full of sadness, I am crying.
I feel lonely and scared.
Do you really love me?
I'm calling you, God.
Please comfort me!

Psalm 88

God, you are so great!
I want to tell everyone I know
about you. I want to sing about
how much you love me,
about the beautiful world you
made. I will sing for you
all day long!

Psalm 89

When I trust in God,
it's like being wrapped
in a warm blanket.
With God on my side,
I am not scared of anything —
not during the day,
not during the night.

Psalm 91

Let's shout out loud
with joy to God!
Because God is a really big God.
He can hold the world
in his hands,
the deep caves,
the mountaintops,
the blue seas —
and you and me too!

Psalm 95

Sing to God a brand-new song,
because he has done
many wonderful things.
Play a trumpet or a horn!
Join the rivers and mountains
in singing praise to God!

Psalm 98

God made us,
and we are all his people.
So we should sing
songs of happiness!
Let's celebrate God's goodness,
his love that will last forever!

Psalm 100

God is so good, so kind,
and he always forgives me.
He loves me like a father
loves his child.
For all of this, I say
thank you, God!

Psalm 103

I praise you, God!
You are like a marvelous king
who wears beautiful, bright robes!
You make the water run in rivers,
and the animals come for a drink.
You make the plants grow,
and we have food to eat.
You open your hands and give us
everything we need.

Psalm 104

My heart is ready, God.
I want to sing.
I want to play music for you
on the strings of a harp
or on a beating drum.
Your love is bigger
than the earth and sky!

Psalm 108

All people everywhere,
all who love God,
let's sing for him
today, tomorrow, and every day!
First thing in the morning
and just before bed,
praise God!

Psalm 113

I love God, because
he listens when I talk to him;
he hears my prayers.
I love God,
because he comforts me
when I am scared.
I thank God for protecting
little children like me.

Psalm 116

Everyone, everywhere,
in every country in the world,
sing a song to God!
Let's praise God together,
for his great love and strength
will last forever.

Psalm 117

When I trust God,
I am strong, like a city
built on top of a big,
tall mountain!
I trust God, because
he protects me
always.

Psalm 125

When I have done
something wrong,
I wait for you to forgive me, God.
I am so sure you will comfort me.
I believe in you, God,
even more than I believe that
tomorrow will come.

Psalm 130

Thank you, God,
you are so good!
Your love never ends.
Thank you, God,
for making the sun!
Your love never ends.
Thank you, God,
for the moon and the stars!
Your love is forever and ever.

Psalm 136

God, you know me so well.
You always know what I'm thinking
and feeling. You know what I am
going to say before I say it!
Even in the night, you can see me —
you know my secrets,
you know my fears.
I praise you for making me
who I am.

Psalm 139

Please God, don't ignore me
when I ask for your help.
I know I can count on you!
Show me the right road to take.
Teach me to obey you and
to do what you want.
You are my God!

Psalm 143

Everyone sing praises to God!
Let's praise God with
guitars, drums, trumpets!
Or tap your feet and dance!
Hallelujah!

Psalm 150

© 2003 Bayard Editions Jeunesse as *Les Psaumes pour les tout-petits*

This edition published in 2008 by
Eerdmans Books for Young Readers,
an imprint of William B. Eerdmans Publishing Co.
2140 Oak Industrial Dr. NE, Grand Rapids, Michigan 49505
P.O. Box 163, Cambridge CB3 9PU U.K.

www.eerdmans.com/youngreaders

Manufactured in China

08 09 10 11 12 13 14 15   8 7 6 5 4 3 2

ISBN 978-0-8028-5322-6 (hardcover : alk. paper)

Library of Congress Cataloging-in-Publication Data

Delval, Marie-Hélène.
[Psaumes pour les tout-petits. English]
Psalms for young children / by Marie-Hélène Delval ; illustrated by Arno.
p. cm.
1. Bible. O.T. Psalms—Paraphrases, English—Juvenile literature. I. Arno. II. Title.
BS1440.D4513 2007
223'.209505--dc22
2006031831

Printed in China by SNP Leefung